INDEPENDENT AND UNOFFICIAL

BTS

K-POP POWER!

CARLTON BOOKS

THIS IS A CARLTON BOOK

Text and design © Carlton Books Limited 2019

Published in 2019 by Carlton Books Limited, an imprint of the Carlton
Publishing Group, 20 Mortimer Street, London W1T 3JW

A catalogue record for this book is available from the British Library.

ISBN: 978-1-78312-463-3

Printed in China

10 9 8 7 6 5 4 3 2 1

Author: Sara Stanford
Designed and packaged by: Dynamo Limited

The publishers would like to thank the following sources for their kind
permission to reproduce the pictures in this book. Key: T=top, C=centre,
B=bottom, L=left, R=right.

Alamy Stock Photo: /Newscom: 32R, 61BL; /Top Photo Corporation: 29B; /
Tsuni USA: 40BL

Getty Images: /Axelle/Bauer-Griffin/FilmMagic: 14-15B; /Bauer-Griffin/GC
Images: 4-5, 13C, 19L, 32L, 37C, 44R, 45TR, 60BC; /Robin Beck/AFP: 24BR; /Choi
Soo-Young/Multi-Bits: 28, 33L, 41B, 61T; /The Chosunilbo JNS/Multi-Bits: 14BL,
19C, 34L, 36L, 37TR, 37L, 41T, 63L, 64; /Chung Sung-Jun: 14L; /Gregg DeGuire/
WireImage: 18L, 18R, 60L; /Santiago Felipe: 24-25C, 27TR, 35TR, 50B, 53TR; /
Steve Granitz/WireImage: 1, 8-9C, 26R, 60R; /Chelsea Guglielmino: 58; /
Raymond Hall/GC Images: 59B; /Han Myung-Gu/WireImage: 9BR, 10-11,
12R, 16-17, 20TR, 26B, 27C, 33B, 35R, 35BL, 39C, 48, 49T, 49BR, 52R, 60BR, 61BR; /
Frazer Harrison: 35TL, 44L, 52L; /ilgan Sports/Multi-Bits: 20-21B, 22-23, 26L, 30-
31, 34BR, 49BL, 50-51T, 63TR; /Jeff Kravitz/FilmMagic: 6-7, 12L, 40R, 53BL, 62; /
Jason LaVeris/FilmMagic: 36R, 38TR, 45BL, 53L, 60TR; /Valerie Macon/AFP:
13BL; /Kevin Mazur/BBMA18/WireImage: 46-47; /Chris Polk/AMA2017: 27L,
29T, 56-57; /Mark Ralston/AFP: 25TR; /Michael Tran/FilmMagic: 19TR; /Yoan
Valat/AFP: 59T, 59R; /Kevin Winter: 13TR, 15R, 33TR, 38BL, 39TL, 52C, 54-55; /Paul
Zimmerman: 33C, 42-43

Shutterstock: /Kim Hee-Chul/EPA-EFE: 25BR, 45L, 51BL; /Yonhap/EPA-EFE: 51BR

Every effort has been made to acknowledge correctly and contact the
source and/or copyright holder of each picture and Carlton Books Limited
apologises for any unintentional errors or omissions that will be corrected in
future editions of this book.

CONTENTS

HELLO

Welcome to your ultimate guide to all things BTS! This is your access-all-areas pass to the planet's biggest pop group and YOUR new favourite band.

INSIDE...

Jam-packed with profiles, photos and fun facts!

For the first time in music history, an Asian band is lighting up the whole world! They write and produce their own songs, and their music is an eclectic mix of everything from hip-hop to breathtaking power ballads. We are, of course, talking about the world's one and only K-pop-phenomenon septet – BTS!

As a mega-fan, you'll know that BTS don't do things by halves. Since forming in 2013, the group has released a string of record-breaking and award-winning EPs, albums and tour trilogies! We're loving that the boys have their own internet and reality TV shows. Their *Bangtan Bomb* YouTube series has clips of their hectic daily lives and tours. It's a chance to hang out with BTS, so what's not to love?

FANS

BTS work hard every day for their fan base, known as the ARMY. This stands for Adorable Representative MC for Youth. Their devoted fans are unstoppable and made BTS the most tweeted-about artists in 2017. Nice work, guys!

FLAVOUR

The band's seven "hella lit" members from oldest to youngest are: Jin, Suga, J-Hope, Rap Monster or RM, Jimin, V and Jungkook. Each of the guys brings their own style and flavour, making BTS a one-of-a-kind seven-piece!

USA

The legendary American talk show host Ellen DeGeneres had BTS on her show in 2017. She compared America's reaction to BTS to Beatlemania in the 1960s.

Millions of followers

BTS were the first South Korean group to achieve 10 million Twitter followers. They became the first K-pop group to perform at the American Music Awards and the first South Korean group to win a Billboard Music Award — all in one year! After their first massive world tour in August 2018, and their 2019 stadium tour, BTS are on a path to sweep the world off its feet. And this is just the beginning for BTS.

Let's find out how much you know about them!

BTS raise the roof with the TV debut of *Fake Love* at the 2018 Billboard Music Awards.

THEY WERE THE FIRST KOREAN ACT TO PERFORM AT THIS ANNUAL AWARD SHOW!

BEFORE THE STARDOM

BTS are the biggest K-pop group in the world, but what's the secret to their success? Let's look back at where BTS began, get the gossip from the auditions and find out all about Bang's BTS vision!

THE NAME

Every band needs a cool name and BTS is exactly that. It is an acronym for the Korean "Bangtan Sonyeondan", which means Bulletproof Boy Scouts. They also go by Beyond the Scene, The Bangtan Boys, or just BTS. So, you can pretty much take your pick.

BEFORE THE BIG BANG

BTS came together at auditions held in Seoul, South Korea between 2010 and 2013. Their mentor is Bang Si-hyuk, the CEO of Big Hit Entertainment. Bang had a vision for them to "become a band that defies prejudices and discriminations against the young generation." He wanted a band with something to say through music that could bring people together no matter what language they speak.

SELECTION

For anyone that thinks BTS are just another boy band, think again. Picking the right boys involved auditioning musicians from all over South Korea in a process that took three years.

"From the beginning I wanted people who knew what they wanted to do, and consequently we found people like that, so I'm happy," commented Bang. "BTS don't just move according to whatever's planned. They create their own music, they manage their schedule.

If they can't do that, the next album won't come out. What they want to wear is also clear."

Rap Monster was the first to audition for Bang. He passed with flying colours. Over the course of two years, Big Hit Entertainment held auditions to find the rest of the members. They had a band to complete. "Suga joined, then J-Hope, who was really popular as a dancer in his hometown. We were the first three!" remembered RM.

COOL FACT ALERT!

It was RM's **RAPPING** at his audition that inspired **BANG** to put together a **HIP-HOP** group.

관광콘서트 2014인천아시아경기대회 D-1년 기념 훈

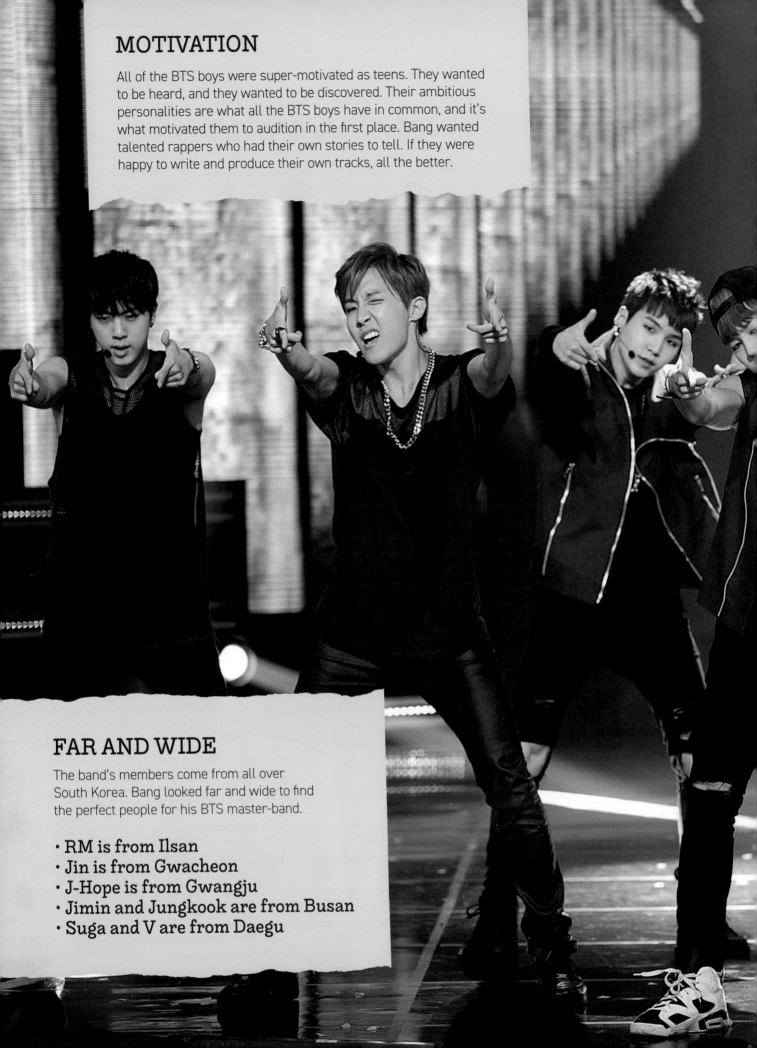

MOTIVATION

All of the BTS boys were super-motivated as teens. They wanted to be heard, and they wanted to be discovered. Their ambitious personalities are what all the BTS boys have in common, and it's what motivated them to audition in the first place. Bang wanted talented rappers who had their own stories to tell. If they were happy to write and produce their own tracks, all the better.

FAR AND WIDE

The band's members come from all over South Korea. Bang looked far and wide to find the perfect people for his BTS master-band.

- RM is from Ilsan
- Jin is from Gwacheon
- J-Hope is from Gwangju
- Jimin and Jungkook are from Busan
- Suga and V are from Daegu

DO YOU KNOW WHY BTS RELEASE THEIR ALBUMS IN THREES? SEVEN MEMBERS MEANS SEVEN STORIES TO TELL. THERE ISN'T ENOUGH SPACE ON ONE ALBUM!

ROOMIES

In 2014, the band prepared to release *2 Cool 4 Skool*. They were living together (and still do!) in a cramped house, sleeping in one room. Although the seven boys were brought together from all over the country, they soon became close. "The seven of us have pushed each other to be the best we can be," revealed RM. "It has made us as close as brothers."

CHATTERBOX

RM is the only fluent English speaker in BTS. He does the most talking in interviews.

KIM SEOK-JIN

Let's hang out with Jin! We all know he's funny, caring and mega-talented, but let's see what else we can find out!

DID YOU KNOW?

Jin is the **OLDEST** member of **BTS!**

BIRTHDAY

4 December 1992

Kim Seok-jin, or just Jin, is one of BTS's four main vocalists. He showcases his awesome voice on the *Wings* solo track *Awake*. These days, Jin is as famous for his love of food as he is for singing. Check out his *Eat Jin* internet TV show!

FUTURE

One day, Jin hopes to focus on acting and hopefully appear in a movie. Right now, his love of music and performing with his best friends comes first.

YOUNG JIN

Jin was born and raised in Anyang City in the Gyeonggi province, then moved to Gwacheon City. Until BTS, Jin always believed that he'd be a farmer, just like the rest of his family. He never imagined that he'd have the opportunity to become a global superstar! At school, Jin couldn't sit still for long, so he didn't really enjoy his studies. His love of acting and film began at high school. "The dream of becoming an actor was born in my second year of high school, after watching Kim Nam Gil-ssi in the drama *Queen Seondeok*," he has revealed. "I was touched and thought that I wanted to make people cry with my acting too. So I studied film at Konkuk University. Three months after starting film school, I was scouted by Big Hit and became a trainee." Big Hit spotted Jin getting off a bus and thought that he had the right look for their new band. At this point, he had no experience of singing or dancing, but that didn't stop him! He was invited to audition and nabbed a spot in the band.

> "PERFORMING IN A CONCERT WAS MY DREAM. I WANTED TO BECOME ONE WITH OUR FANS THROUGH OUR MUSIC."

HIS FAVE COLOUR IS BLUE

WE JUST LOVE JIN'S MOTTO:

"Live life with no worries."

BIG HIT TRAINEE

The next step for Jin was to become a Big Hit trainee (Bang Si-hyuk's way of making sure all members were ready to be part of the band). At this point, Jin wasn't very confident – he didn't think he could dance or write songs. His BTS brothers soon changed all of that and helped him become more comfortable performing and expressing himself. "My interest in music started after I met the members," Jin recalled. "Thanks to the influence from our members, I'm now continuing to write songs. Even though they aren't at the level of being put into albums yet, I get good responses."

Ha! Ha! HA!

Jin is forever telling "dad" jokes.

2 COOL 4 SKOOL

"TEAMWORK MAKES THE DREAM WORK."
-RM

Everyone knows BTS from their hit 2015 single *I NEED U* and their 2016 album *Wings*, but they first began making waves back in 2013. Their debut album, *2 Cool 4 Skool*, broke down barriers and launched the K-pop phenomenon.

TRACK LISTING:

♫ Intro: 2 Cool 4 Skool *(feat. DJ Friz)*

♫ We Are Bulletproof Pt.2

♫ Skit: Circle Room Talk

♫ No More Dream

♫ Interlude

♫ I Like It

♫ Outro: Circle Room Cypher

♫ Skit: On the Start Line *(hidden track)*

♫ Path *(hidden track)*

RM SPOKE AT THE UNITED NATIONS...
"NO MATTER WHO YOU ARE, WHERE YOU'RE FROM, YOUR SKIN COLOUR, GENDER IDENTITY: SPEAK YOURSELF."

Rap-pop phenomenon BTS kicked things off with their *Skool* trilogy of albums. Their debut record *2 Cool 4 Skool* was followed by 2013's *O!RUL8,2?* and *Skool Luv Affair* EPs. The *Skool* trilogy is packed with lyrics and tracks that reflect the issues and everyday lives of teens. BTS set out to write lyrics that really meant something to their young fans. They focused on themes important to that age group, such as bullying, parents, exams and young love.

"We tried to relate with listeners who are of our age group and brought up topics that we could think about together," explained Suga. "The pain and uncertainty associated with being young, and the wrong ideas that can form during that age were issues we wanted to put in our songs." J-Hope added: "BTS makes music to speak to the feelings of teenagers. To stop against the prejudice and oppression of the world for teenagers."

BTS's first single to set the music scene alight was *No More Dream*. The song was released in South Korea on 13 June 2013, the day after *2 Cool 4 Skool* dropped. It has been described as "a rebellious rejection of Korean traditionalism". The track reached No.14 in the Billboard World Digital Charts, and it would be one of the last times a song of theirs would place so low in the charts. Because the song was distributed by the independent record label Big Hit Entertainment, it struggled to reach a larger audience. Even so, Bang knew that the BTS boys were exactly what audiences needed, and they needed them now!

Following the release of *2 Cool 4 Skool*, BTS began starring in their own SBS MTV variety show called *Rookie King: Channel Bangtan*. This was the boys' first ever reality TV show. They also started broadcasting their own show called *American Hustle Life*, which is all about the seven band members finding their way in American hip-hop. Some familiar faces crop up along the way, such as US hip-hop star Coolio.

FUN FACT

The album has **9** tracks, but **2** of them are **HIDDEN**.

FUN FACT

BTS DOLLS ARE COMING!
Thanks to Mattel, we will soon be able to grab our own pocket-sized BTS fashion dolls. Which will you pick?

K-pop started in the 1990s in South Korea! It blends popular styles of Asian and Western music.

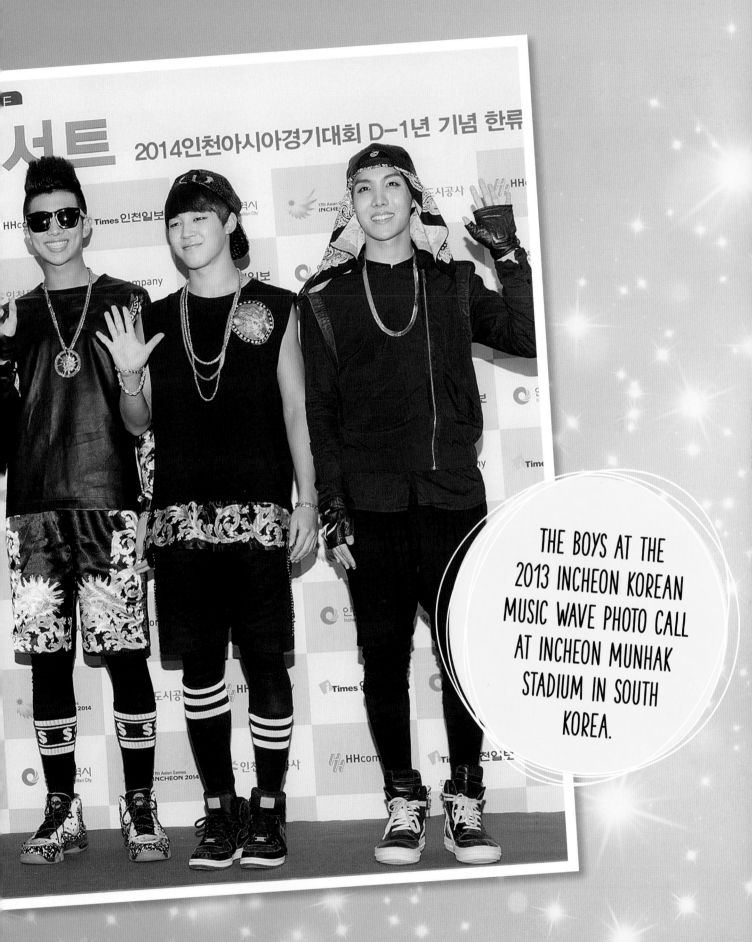

THE BOYS AT THE 2013 INCHEON KOREAN MUSIC WAVE PHOTO CALL AT INCHEON MUNHAK STADIUM IN SOUTH KOREA.

MIN YOON-GI

Let's hang out with BTS's lead rapper, Suga. This songwriter and award-winning record producer has a lot to say, and we can't wait to hear him!

BIRTHDAY
9 March 1993

SUGA IS A PROUD SUPPORTER OF LGBTQ RIGHTS AND TALKS ABOUT THIS A LOT IN INTERVIEWS.

RAP MASTER

Suga was born in Daegu, which is the fourth biggest city in South Korea. He grew up there until he came to Seoul. "When I was young, I was pretty much an ordinary kid... until I started to be interested in music in the fifth year of elementary school." This was when hip-hop began filling Suga's ears, and he had the idea of becoming a hip-hop star! Since then, Min Yoon-gi, or Suga, has become a total rhyme and rap master. It's no surprise as he's been practising for a long time! "I have been writing rhymes and lyrics since I was a kid," Suga explained. "They are all the little minor feelings and thoughts that go through my mind. I shuffle them a year or so later, and they become great lyrics for songs."

Motionless Min
On his days off, Suga likes doing absolutely nothing! He's been nicknamed Motionless Min.

GLOSS

Did you know that Suga once went by the name of Gloss? It's true! He used to write beats in Daegu (his hometown) and give them away to local artists. "Back then," Suga recalled, "no one around me liked hip-hop. It is extremely popular in Korea now, but when I first started listening to it, no one else was." In his first year of high school, Suga joined a hip-hop crew called D-town and began rapping properly. He discovered the local Daegu underground hip-hop scene in his teens and met like-minded people. It was here that Suga's life changed.

SUGA RELEASED HIS SOLO MIXTAPE CALLED AGUST D. CHECK IT OUT!

He's been making music since he was a little kid!

"I knew Big Hit was holding an audition in Daegu," Suga said. He saw a flyer advertising a competition called Hit it. He didn't really know what to expect, but he decided to go for it anyway! "I auditioned and I was told that I was accepted the next day. I wanted to debut and become a singer doing my music as a trainee. There was never a moment when I didn't have a dream to do that." He's not interested in being a celebrity – he just wants to be the best rapper and the best producer out there. We believe in you, Suga!

> "IN ADDITION TO BEING WHAT WE ARE AS BTS, WE WANTED TO BRING SOME CHANGES AND WE ACTUALLY WANTED TO EVOLVE AS A GROUP. WE WANTED TO SHOW OUR MANY COLOURS, BUT WE STILL WANT TO CONSOLE AND GIVE HOPE TO OTHERS."
>
> -Suga

DARK & WILD

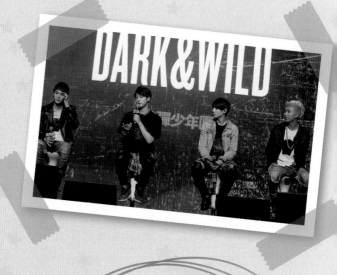

With BTS's first *Skool* trilogy out in the wild, it was time for them to begin the next chapter of their career – the *Youth* trilogy.

EVOLUTION

BTS were growing up alongside their fans, and their music changed to show that. They began producing more experimental and high-energy dance music. In 2014 the boys began their *Youth* trilogy with their first full-length album, *Dark & Wild*. The adventure was only just beginning.

> "COMPARED TO OTHER GROUPS, OUR GROUP IS QUITE HEAVY ON THE LYRICS... SINCE THERE ARE A LOT OF THINGS WE WANT TO SAY."
>
> -RM

TRACK LISTING:

🎵 Intro: What Am I To You

🎵 Danger

🎵 War of Hormone

🎵 Hip-hop Lover

🎵 Let Me Know

🎵 Rain

🎵 BTS Cypher Pt. 3: Killer (*ft. Supreme Boi*)

🎵 Interlude: What Are You Doing

🎵 Can You Turn Off Your Phone?

🎵 Blanket Kick

🎵 24/7 = Heaven

🎵 Look Here

🎵 Second Grade

🎵 Outro: Does That Make Sense?

THE BOYS WANTED A HIT!

2 Cool 4 Skool had been an introduction to the band's personalities, but it was time to mix things up. With their *Skool* years behind them, BTS decided to take their music in a new direction.

In 2014, BTS wrote and recorded more upbeat tracks. It was time to dance! "BTS music is based on hip-hop and pop music in general, because all the members grew up listening to famous hip-hop artists as well as pop vocalists, even before the debut. It was definitely very hip-hop back in 2013, and the style kind of evolved as we grew up listening to and experiencing many different genres of music the last couple of years," explained RM.

It was an exciting time for BTS. They were enjoying the fact that Bang was giving them oodles of creative freedom. RM decided to write about leaving his teenage years behind him, recalling how he "wanted to express the thoughts of men in their early twenties." They decided that their album would be called *Dark & Wild*. It would celebrate the reckless and carefree youth that we live before having to grow up.

Dark & Wild has two distinct halves with an interlude in between. The track list was written to tell a story, so it's best to listen to the songs in order, from the start to the end. The album's lead single is called *Danger*.

POWER OF YOUTUBE

BTS's fan base really stepped up a gear with this album, and it was all thanks to sharing their music on YouTube (and BTS's awesomeness of course!). When the boys performed live, they played to chanting crowds who even knew the words to all of their songs.

WORLD TOUR

From this moment on, the band's fan base grew and grew. They went on a world tour just as *The Most Beautiful Moment in Life, Pt. 2* EP hit the Top Ten in international music charts, including Billboard's World Albums chart – the first K-pop band EVER to do this! RM understood why BTS were making waves where other K-pop bands failed. It was all about the brotherly bonds between the band.

Dark & Wild debuted at No. 2 on the Gaon charts in South Korea. It was the band's highest chart placement so far – BTS's gamble of a new musical direction had paid off. Six months later, *I NEED U* from *The Most Beautiful Moment in Life, Pt. 1* EP was released. This was when their lives changed forever. "BTS as a group took off with the success of our hit single *I NEED U*," RM told *Time* magazine. The video got more than a million views on social media in 24 hours. Due to the song's success, they went to KCON in 2015 – a K-pop music festival in America and Europe. "We didn't realize we were becoming famous until the KCON festival," said RM.

All in black and white – these guys are always on fleek!

BTS ARE ALL ABOUT THEIR FANS. THEY ENJOY INTERACTING WITH THEM ON SOCIAL MEDIA AND LOVE LIVE-STREAMING SO THEIR FOLLOWERS CAN KEEP UP WITH THEIR EVERY MOVE!

BTS WOW THE CROWDS WITH THEIR PERFORMANCE AT ILCHI ART HALL IN SEOUL, SOUTH KOREA IN JUNE 2013.

WANT TO JOIN THE BTS ARMY?

Then it's your lucky day! Here's our guide to being a number one fan. Get ready to jot down these top tips, and you'll be part of the ARMY in no time.

1

Polish up your dance skills!

Have fun coming up with awesome moves. You could even learn some moves from the BTS YouTube channel!

2

Get to know their albums.

No matter what mood you're in, a BTS song (or five!) will ALWAYS do the trick.

3

Come up with your own BTS name so you're ready to join the crew.

Do you have a nickname that you like? If not, you can make up your own. It could be your initials, or perhaps you could base it on your favourite animal, song or place.

4 Keep this book close to you at all times!

That way, you'll be sure to know all there is to know about the best boy band on the planet.

5 Get some pals on board.

Do your friends love BTS, too? Together you could form your own ARMY for hanging out, chatting about BTS and listening to their music. The possibilities are endless!

6 Share the love.

Their positive vibe is what makes BTS so loveable, so follow their lead and spread their message to everyone you meet.

7 Keep being you.

If there's one thing that the BTS boys are all about, it's being yourself. Why fit in when you can be an individual!

JUNG HO-SEOK

He's positive, he's uber-friendly AND he's a sensational dancer! What's not to love? Come on, it's time for us to get to know J-Hope a little better.

BIRTHDAY
18 February 1994

HIS SOLO SONG *MAMA* IS DEDICATED TO HIS MOTHER. AWW!

★ CLOSE CALL ★
Legend has it that J-Hope nearly got left out of BTS for not being the right fit! Can you believe it? Luckily, RM persuaded Big Hit that BTS needed J-Hope. Phew!

GUESS WHAT...
J-Hope is the **ONLY** member of **BTS** with **ZERO** ear-piercings.

STREET DANCE

Before joining BTS in 2012, J-Hope was part of an underground street dance squad called Neuron. This was where J-Hope found his signature move! "While promoting with my underground street dance team, I did a lot of popping," revealed J-Hope in 2013. "In popping, there's another sub-genre called boogaloos and that was the one I did the most. I got a lot of prizes and performed a lot. Rap Monster rapped underground; I danced." J-Hope was born in Gwangju and grew up watching Western music videos on YouTube. "When I was a little kid, I simply loved music and enjoyed expressing myself with my body. Everyone liked me when I went up on the stage at a talent search in elementary school, and that's when I decided to become a music artist."

AS A KID, J-HOPE WAS A KEEN TENNIS PLAYER.

HIS CLOSEST BANDMATE IS JIN. HERE'S HOW JIN DESCRIBES HIM:

"He's a kid who's just all hope. He makes anyone bright when he's with them – he laughs even when there's no reason."

Following his time in Neuron, J-Hope built up a reputation as a dancer. In 2008 he even won a national dance competition in South Korea! "While enrolling at Korea Arts School, there were lots of trainees coming from different districts," J-Hope recalled. "When I debuted with Bangtan, my friends said, 'J-Hope, is he the one from that dance academy in Gwangju?' That's how famous I was!"

THE BEST

Dancing was J-Hope's dream! Like his bandmates, he had to work super-hard to prove himself to Hit Entertainment. "My goal was always clear. To stand on stage, to become the best," J-Hope confided. "But first, I needed to survive. The trainee period was a constant cycle of having to survive. When one person entered, one person would have to leave. I had to withstand that."

JUNG HO-SEOK, OR J-HOPE, IS BTS'S RAY OF SUNSHINE, AS WELL AS THEIR BEST DANCER (MAYBE!). WE LOVE THAT HE ADOPTED HIS STAGE NAME BECAUSE HE WANTED TO BE A SOURCE OF LIGHT AND HOPE TO HIS FANS. SWEET, RIGHT?

WINGS

The release of *Wings* brought worldwide success for BTS! It also brought them an ever-growing ARMY of fans. BTS-mania was taking over the world.

WINGS WAS THE FIRST KOREAN ALBUM TO MAKE IT INTO THE UK ALBUM CHARTS.

TRACK LISTING:

🎵 Intro: Boy Meets Evil

🎵 Blood Sweat & Tears

🎵 Begin

🎵 Lie

🎵 Stigma

🎵 First Love

🎵 Reflection

🎵 MAMA

🎵 Awake

🎵 Lost

🎵 BTS Cypher 4

🎵 Am I Wrong

🎵 21st Century Girl

🎵 Two! Three! (Wishing for Better Days)

🎵 Interlude: Wings

In 2016, *Wings* became the first K-pop album to crack the Top 30 in the American Billboard charts. It was just what BTS and Big Hit had been waiting for! All of the hard work was worth it. "I don't think the successful result of *Wings* was expected," admitted Bang, "but I don't think the results were a matter of luck."

Nobody really expected BTS to be SO successful outside of Korea – even the boys! "I was shocked to see our name in the Hot 100 chart," RM said. "In the United States, a song that breaks into the Top 40 is considered a nationwide hit, you know. The fact that we were in the Top 30 was just unbelievable."

The *Wings* album features seven solo tracks, and it is all about growing up. It has a more mature sound than the *Youth* trilogy. On this album, the band were free to write and share their own stories. It was a chance for each member to reveal more of their personality to the world. Suga explained of the lead single, *Blood Sweat & Tears*, "The song relays an optimistic determination to use our wings to go far, even if we are met with temptations in life."

"EACH SONG ON *WINGS* REFLECTS THE HARDSHIPS WE OVERCAME. IT REALLY REPRESENTS THE PERSONS WE ARE."

-RM

TRANSFORMATION!

Each of the band's solo songs show off their different musical styles. The tracks highlight how much each member has changed since joining BTS – what a journey they've all been on!

Wings stands out because all seven members are equal. RM was originally the leader, but on *Wings* each member stepped up to the mic with something to say. "The big thing about creating our universe is expandability," Suga commented, talking about their constantly evolving sound and style. "Because the universe we create draws from our personal lives and interests, we can expand it as much as we want and it's not alien for us. Having that allows us more diversity in the stories we can tell and the music we can make."

NO LIE

Jimin's *Lie* was a big hit on the iTunes download charts.

WINGS

Their ARMY fan base is growing day by day with no sign of things slowing up. Next stop – global domination!

BTS ARE AS FAMOUS FOR THEIR CHOREOGRAPHY
AS THEY ARE FOR THEIR MUSIC.

KIM NAM-JOON

All bands need a captain, and BTS's captain is RM. Here's everything you need to know about the band's lead songwriter, producer and rapper.

BIRTHDAY
12 September 1994

HE'S THE TALLEST MEMBER IN THE BAND AT 1.8 M.

Roooaaar!
RM stands for Rap Monster.

STYLE ICON
When it comes to fashion, RM has oodles of style. He has had so many cool looks over the years.

Runch Randa
Before BTS, Rap Monster went by his underground rapper name, Runch Randa!

RISING STAR

RM was 13 years old when he started writing song lyrics. He was part of the underground rap crew DaeNamHyup. Suga and J-Hope were also on the underground scene, and together they were the first three members to join BTS. "We came together with a common dream to write, dance and produce music," RM said.

It was clear from the start that RM was a star waiting for his chance to shine. He was the first member to be discovered by Big Hit Entertainment. "Back in 2010, I was introduced to Bang." recalls RM, "I was an underground rapper and only 16 years old, a freshman at high school. Bang thought I had potential as a rapper and lyricist."

RM IS REALLY SMART. HIS IQ IS 148.

SPEAK OUT

An **INSPIRATIONAL** figure to millions, RM speaks to fans at **KCON 2016.**

RM has kept up his song writing and has built up quite a back catalogue! There's no doubt that his unique lyrics and melodies have helped shaped BTS.

"I started this because I wanted to say something. There was a message inside me and I wanted to spread it as music," the rapper revealed. "But we're just a normal group of boys from humble backgrounds who have a lot of passion and a dream to be famous."

ENJOY THE RIDE

RM wants to make sure BTS enjoy the ride they're on, while being taken seriously. "Through the prism of my songs I constantly observe society and I want to be a person who can have a better, positive impact on other people. It will always be important to keep working hard, dancing better, writing better songs, touring and setting an example."

"PEOPLE LOVE ME FOR WHAT I AM. THAT'S HOW I MANAGE TO BE ME AND BE HUMBLE AS A HUMAN BEING."
-RM

TOP 11: BAND MEMBER QUOTES

BTS are known for spreading positivity, and their lyrics never fail to bring joy to their fans. We've picked out 11 of the best things BTS have said or sung, especially for you!

JIMIN

Go on your path, even if you live for a day.

I want people to get positive energy from our music.

Never give up on a dream that you've been chasing almost all of your life.

SUGA

Life is tough, and things don't always work out well, but we should be brave and go on with our lives.

34

JUNGKOOK

BTS

The only time you should ever look back is to see how far you've come.

You will regret someday if you don't do your best now. Don't think it's too late, but keep working on it. It may take time, but there's nothing that gets worse due to practising. So practise.

J-HOPE

RAP MONSTER

Keep every promise you can make and make every promise you can keep.

The music helped me sympathize with our young generation and also empathize with them. I'd like to create and write more music that represents them.

Happiness is not something that you have to achieve, you can still feel happy during the process of achieving something.

Teamwork makes the dream work...

I think the biggest love is the love for oneself, so if you want to love others, you should love yourself first.

PARK JI-MIN

The final member to join BTS was Jimin! He's known for being the sweetest member of the band. He is full of energy and is always dancing! There is NEVER a dull moment when Jimin's about.

If Jimin could have any superpower, it would be to talk to animals.

BIRTHDAY
13 October 1995

Besides dance, Jimin also liked **ART, PE, MATHS** and **CHEMISTRY** at school.

SUPPORT
Jimin is thankful to the ARMY for attending the 2017 American Music Awards. This prestigious industry event was held at LA's Microsoft Theatre.

JIMIN IS A TOTAL PERFECTIONIST! ESPECIALLY WHEN IT COMES TO HIS DANCE CHOREOGRAPHY AND SINGING.

TOP STUDENT

Park Ji-Min, or Jimin, was born in the city of Busan. He discovered his love of performing while he was at school and practised every day after his studies! Through hard work, Jimin built up his confidence and got into the local dance academy, Busan High School of Arts. He became one of the school's top modern dance students, and his teachers encouraged him to audition for Big Hit Entertainment.

TRAINEE LIFE

When the chance to join Big Hit Entertainment came along, Jimin moved from his hometown to live in Seoul. "The most difficult part of the trainee life was the uncertainty of my future," revealed Jimin. "I was the last to be added to the group, that's why I practise so hard. I got anxious when I heard 'you might get eliminated this time', so I wanted to do my best with practising."

"JIMIN IS A REAL PIECE OF CUTENESS, LIKE THE YOUNGEST IN THE FAMILY."
-V

STYLE FILE

Jimin isn't afraid to show his **FASHIONABLE** side!

"If I practised until 4am, I would sleep a bit and go practise singing at 6am for an hour and then go to school. This routine continued for about a year. At the time, I've never thought I could become a member of BTS. I was chosen, but only as a substitute member. The rest of the chosen members said, 'We want to debut with Jimin,' and that became my strength."

Now Jimin had the moves and the perfectionist attitude to boot! This meant that his time as a trainee was the shortest of all the members – under a year! Jimin was the final piece of the puzzle and the line-up was complete. "I was so excited when we debuted," Jimin remembers. "After the showcase we all cried." The group had their first taste of worldwide success with the *Wings* album, and Jimin's track *Lie* became the stand-out solo track. It showcased Jimin's vocal skills and delighted their fans!

"I WOULD LOVE IT IF THEY REMEMBERED US AS BOYS WHO ALWAYS WANTED TO SHOW THEIR SINCERITY AND THEIR SINCEREST SIDE."
-JIMIN

As a student, Jimin's dreams for his future career changed daily!

LOVE YOURSELF: TEAR

This album was a turning point for BTS. It was the start of their second chapter and their rise to icon status!

BREAKING AMERICA

Wings had made it into the Top 30 of the US Billboard charts and left American fans wanting more. BTS were breaking records, language barriers and stereotypes! They were like no other band in the US charts, and that's what everyone loved about them. They had made their mark on America, and *Love Yourself: Tear* couldn't come quick enough!

BTS strike a pose at the American Music Awards in 2017.

DJ MAGIC

Next, the boys decided to work with Steve Aoki, a world-famous DJ. Aoki worked his trap-beat magic on the song *Mic Drop* from 2017's *Love Yourself: Her* EP. This got BTS their first Top 40 hit single in the US. All of a sudden, America wanted anything and everything BTS. Even the boys' back catalogue of songs were climbing the global charts!

The world listens! BTS proudly accept the Top Social Artist award at the 2018 Billboard Music Awards.

LOVE YOURSELF: TEAR

The album was released in May 2018 — the same month as their incredible win at the Billboard Music Awards! The band were catapulted to a whole new level of fame. Suddenly, a boy band rapping in Korean was knocking American artists off the US Billboard charts!

GUESS WHAT?

The **ARMY** voted for the **#BTSBBMAS** hashtag more than 320 million times!

The winners of Top Social Artist at the 2018 Billboard Music Awards: BTS!

Looking playful at the 5th Gaon Chart K-pop Awards in 2016.

TRACK LISTING:

♫ Intro: Singularity

♫ Fake Love

♫ The Truth Untold

♫ 134340

♫ Paradise

♫ Love Maze

♫ Magic Shop

♫ Airplane pt.2

♫ Anpanman

♫ So What

♫ Outro: Tear

TAKING HOME TROPHIES

When BTS collected the award for Top Social Artist at the 2018 Billboard Awards, the boys were in shock. "Everyone in the group was very nervous," the band said of the night. "When BTS's name was read out, nobody could believe it!"

RM gave a speech, which he read out on stage: "We won the Top Social Artist Award thanks to the dedication of our ARMY around the world. Our honour and gratitude must go directly to them." By taking the Top Social Artist award, BTS broke Justin Bieber's six-year winning streak. It may have been unexpected to BTS, but the ARMY knew their favourite band would take the prize.

LOVE YOURSELF: ANSWER ♪

Up next we have the final record of the *Love Yourself* trilogy! *Love Yourself: Answer* marked the end of one chapter for BTS and the beginning of another — the boys were heading out on tour.

This record was released in not one, not two, not three, but FOUR different versions, named S, E, L and F. The lead single *Idol* sums up the album, mixing traditional Korean culture and music with trap beats and electronic dance music. The song, naturally, broke the internet within hours of its release. "The song has the message of loving one's true self no matter what others say," said J-Hope.

BTS BREAK THE INTERNET

BTS made history with *Idol*. In 2018 it was the fastest music video of the year to reach over 100 million views.

REMIX IT!

Just one version of the song wasn't enough for BTS. They dropped a remixed version of *Idol* with the help of one of their OWN idols – US rap superstar Nicki Minaj. "We thought the song would come alive with Nicki Minaj's rapping, so we sent a request," said RM. "Nicki Minaj's side accepted, so it came to be!"

The music video set the YouTube record for most views in 24 hours. It beat Taylor Swift's video for *Look What You Made Me Do*, with more than 45 million views! It's a cheeky and energetic video that brings together Korean traditions with the modern day. We reckon it deserves every single view.

SEVEN
This album includes seven incredible new songs!

"With our *Love Yourself* series we wanted to show the emotional development of a young man through love," explained RM. "We tried to send the message that loving yourself is where true love begins. For *Love Yourself: Answer* we have seven brand-new tracks. We've put our Korean traditional sound, performance and traditional Korean choreography into the videos too. This album is a celebration of our culture."

BOYS ON TOUR
This was their final release before BTS set out on their *Love Yourself* tour.

SMASHED IT!
Naturally, *Love Yourself: Answer* smashed as many records as those that came before it!

SO MUCH SWAG!
HERE ARE OUR FAVOURITE
LADS STRUTTING THEIR
STUFF AT KCON 2016 IN

TOP OF THE TWITTER CHARTS

BTS were THE most re-tweeted artist in 2016. The ARMY certainly have fast fingers!

KIM TAE-HYUNG

CLICK, CLICK
Art and photography are two of V's passions.

V's a singer, songwriter, actor AND producer. How does he find the time to fit it all in? Get to know this fashion-loving, fussy eater!

BIRTHDAY
30 December 1995

CHILDHOOD

Growing up, V was raised by his grandmother among a family of farmers. "I was born in Daegu, the same place as Suga," V recalled in an interview. "At elementary school, I was a curious kid who wanted to do everything. I lived in the countryside, so I didn't imagine doing anything except for farming in the future, but I still thought I had to study hard. That changed after I fell in love with music. By the end of my sixth year at school, I had the dream of becoming a singer. It was my first time having a certain dream."

V's dream was to pursue music, so he started with saxophone lessons at school. His Dad had always encouraged V to follow his passions. "I started preparing for my dream from my first year of middle school. My father asked 'What do you want to do later?' and I answered 'I want to become a singer.' My father used to dream of becoming an actor, so after hearing my answer, he told me very seriously, 'If you want to become a singer, you have to learn at least one instrument.' So I learned saxophone for three years. It looks cool, but my lips hurt a lot and it was heavy too – it was quite hard."

AUDITION

V went along to support a friend who was auditioning for Big Hit Entertainment. Someone from the Big Hit team saw V in the waiting room and asked him to audition, too. Before he knew it, V was walking into the audition room to face the panel. "I danced, rapped and showed my voice imitations and gags at the audition. I thought I would fail for sure but then they contacted me saying I passed. I thought it was a lie. I was the only one to pass that day in Daegu."

V CAN SPEAK 3 LANGUAGES – KOREAN, JAPANESE AND ENGLISH!

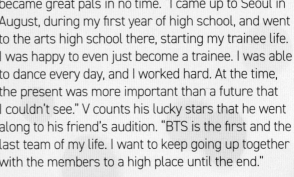

HANDY!
V is ambidextrous, so he is both left and right handed.

Unlike the others, V wasn't known on the underground music scene. At first, V being in the band was kept secret! "After getting to debut, my existence was hidden until the end. I was the secret weapon! Because of that, there were times I couldn't say I was going to debut and was upset," revealed V. "The other members all had schedules, only I stayed behind at the dorm and rested. So, when I was revealed, I was extremely happy. I was so happy thinking 'My dream since the sixth year of elementary school finally came true!'"

V met the rest of the band as a trainee, and they became great pals in no time. "I came up to Seoul in August, during my first year of high school, and went to the arts high school there, starting my trainee life. I was happy to even just become a trainee. I was able to dance every day, and I worked hard. At the time, the present was more important than a future that I couldn't see." V counts his lucky stars that he went along to his friend's audition. "BTS is the first and the last team of my life. I want to keep going up together with the members to a high place until the end."

BTS TAKE HOME THE AWARD FOR TOP SOCIAL ARTIST AT THE 2018 BILLBOARD MUSIC AWARDS IN LAS VEGAS.

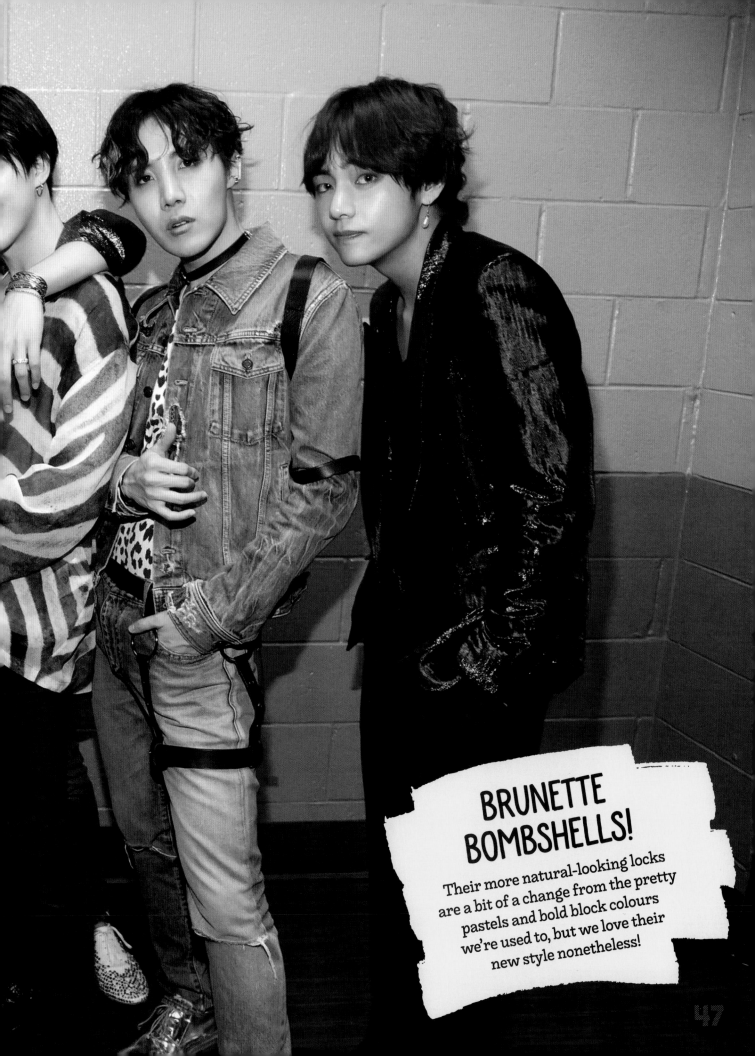

BRUNETTE BOMBSHELLS!

Their more natural-looking locks are a bit of a change from the pretty pastels and bold block colours we're used to, but we love their new style nonetheless!

EVOLUTION OF BTS

DESIGNER STYLE
BTS adore Gucci. Fancy!

Everyone knows that BTS LOVE fashion! These boys are forever experimenting with style and colour in new and exciting ways — and we're not just talking about their clothes! BTS are total perfectionists when it comes to their style, and we've picked seven stand-out moments to celebrate. Bizarre or brilliant? YOU decide...

BTS at the 3rd Gaon Chart K-pop Awards in 2014. The magnificent seven look, well, magnificent! These guys clearly know how to work the monochrome look.

Here they are at their very first Incheon Korean Music Wave photo call in 2013. This would mark the start of BTS-mania. The boys are a vision of black and gold bling. Their muted hair colours show that BTS mean business.

"IT'S SOMETIMES JUST UNBELIEVABLE: PARTIALLY MAYBE IT WAS A BIT OF LUCK. WE DO OUR BEST AND KEEP WORKING NO MATTER WHAT. THE FANS SUPPORTED US SO MUCH, THEY LOVE US. WE'D LIKE TO GO HIGHER FROM HERE."

-JUNGKOOK

Showcasing their album *Dark & Wild* in Seoul, South Korea on 19 August 2014. BTS look stylish but rebellious with their denim-and-leather look. Check out the chains to match.

The septet donned snappy suits for their performance on SBS MTV's *The Show* in 2015. Simple, but oh so effective!

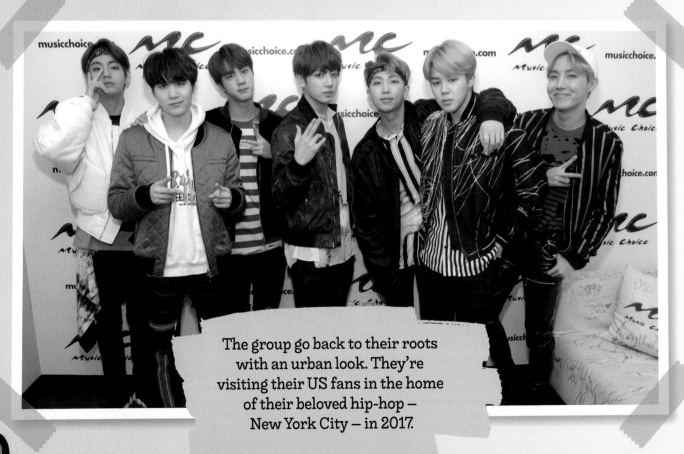

The group go back to their roots with an urban look. They're visiting their US fans in the home of their beloved hip-hop — New York City — in 2017.

SO sophisticated! This smart attire can only mean one thing... they've gone to the 2018 Golden Disc Awards.

From hip-hop to pop stars! Once again, BTS showcase a new look at the *Love Yourself: Her* press conference in 2018.

51

JEON JUNG-KOOK

Up next, it's Jungkook — he's BTS's main vocalist, lead dancer and rapper. Is there anything he can't do?

Gaming
In his free time, this dude loves gaming!

Jung Kook

BIRTHDAY
1 September 1997

BABY OF THE GROUP

Jeon Jung-kook, or Jungkook, is BTS's maknae (which means youngest member). In K-pop, the youngest in the group gets extra attention. But when you're as talented, funny and handsome as Jungkook, you'd expect that anyway! Before stardom, Jungkook was at Baek Yang Middle School, and then Seoul School of Performing Arts High School. Even at school his talents shone through.

"In seventh grade, I dreamt of becoming a singer after listening to G-Dragon's songs," Jungkook recalled. The aspiring star immediately chased that dream and was in-demand long before his BTS showcase. It all started when he auditioned for *Superstar K*, the South Korean talent show. He got as far as the final elimination round and caught the attention of Big Hit Entertainment. "I got eliminated anyway. Even if I had passed, I think I would have chosen Big Hit," Jungkook said. At 12 years old, he signed up with the agency. He was a trainee for three years before he debuted with his BTS brothers.

BY JUST 15, JUNGKOOK HAD DEBUTED WITH BTS.

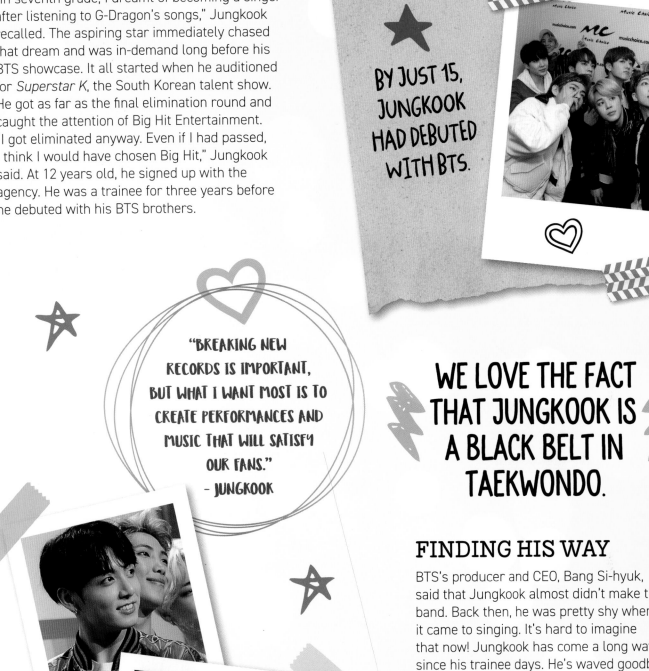

"BREAKING NEW RECORDS IS IMPORTANT, BUT WHAT I WANT MOST IS TO CREATE PERFORMANCES AND MUSIC THAT WILL SATISFY OUR FANS."
- JUNGKOOK

WE LOVE THE FACT THAT JUNGKOOK IS A BLACK BELT IN TAEKWONDO.

FINDING HIS WAY

BTS's producer and CEO, Bang Si-hyuk, said that Jungkook almost didn't make the band. Back then, he was pretty shy when it came to singing. It's hard to imagine that now! Jungkook has come a long way since his trainee days. He's waved goodbye to his stagefright and performed on *The Ellen DeGeneres Show* and at heaps of high profile events. "I was never nervous," Jungkook exclaimed. "That's because I believe in our fans. In those moments, I felt I made the right choice to pursue a singing career, so why be scared?"

RM's mad skills as a rapper and producer inspire Jungkook. And RM has plenty of good stuff to say about Jungkook, too: "He's good-looking, and he has a lot of ambition... He's good at everything." We totally agree with you, RM!

K-POP PHENOMENON

BTS-mania is taking over the world, and we've got the facts, stats and numbers to prove it!

The band

4
MAIN SINGERS

3
LEAD RAPPERS

7
DANCERS (YEP, THAT'S ALL OF THEM!)

@BTS_twt was the FIRST EVER Korean Twitter account to reach 10 million followers.

2 The number of times BTS appear in the *Guinness World Records* 2019 edition.

Fake Love The music video had 35.9 million views in its first 24 hours.

***Time* magazine** named BTS on their list of the 25 most influential people on the Internet in 2018, for the second year running.

ARMY WON A 2018 RADIO DISNEY MUSIC AWARD FOR 'FIERCEST FANS'.

6	**4**	**3**	**5**
STUDIO ALBUMS	COMPILATION ALBUMS	SINGLE ALBUMS	EXTENDED PLAY ALBUMS

BTS official social media accounts

Over 16 MILLION subscribers to their YouTube channel @BANGTANTV

More than 16 MILLION Instagram followers @bts.bighitofficial

19.3 MILLION Twitter followers @BTS_twt

Awards
BTS were the first K-Pop band to win a Billboard Music Award – voted for by their fans!

Love Yourself: Her
was number one in the iTunes album charts in 73 countries.

12-15 hours
... that's how long BTS practised for their debut performance!

America
BTS are the first EVER Korean pop group to top the US album charts.

BTS GET IT ON PERFORMING *DNA* AT THE 2017 AMERICAN MUSIC AWARDS AT THE MICROSOFT THEATER IN LOS ANGELES.

GUESS WHAT?

BTS joined Ed Sheeran and Ariana Grande on the best-selling artists list for 2018!

BURN THE STAGE: THE MOVIE

Just when you thought that being a BTS fan couldn't get any better, they go and release a movie!

"WE'RE PROUD THAT EVERYTHING WE DO IS GIVING OFF LIGHT." –J-HOPE

BTS's first feature-length film, called *Burn the Stage*, was released in November 2018. If you haven't had a chance to see it yet, what are you waiting for? It's your chance to get up close and personal with the planet's favourite Korean boy band!

WHAT A YEAR!

The movie topped off an epic 2018 for BTS. It was the year they became a global music superpower.

RM had released his second mixtape called *Mono*, which received lots of love. BTS had performed *I'm Fine* and *Idol* on one of the most-watched US talk shows, *The Tonight Show with Jimmy Fallon*. Plus, they'd announced their English track *Waste It on Me* with Steve Aoki. The boys performed at London's O2 Arena and appeared on *The Graham Norton Show* in the UK.

But it was the first trailer for *Burn the Stage* that truly sent the ARMY into mega-meltdown. This was the moment everyone was waiting for – a movie! The ARMY knew that a BTS feature-length film had to happen. After all, their music videos are like mini movies, and we all know they love acting...

Their debut movie is not entirely new content. It's actually clips taken from their YouTube Red series of the same name. The access-all-areas docu-series began in March 2017. The footage takes you behind the scenes of BTS's Wings tour. It shows the group's dedication to one another as brothers, as well as their dedication to music and their beloved fans.

YOUTUBE

BTS's eight-part YouTube series, *Burn the Stage*, was turned into an 85-minute movie. It's subtitled, so that fans can enjoy it no matter where they live in the world. What's more, it includes added performances, interviews and extra behind-the-scenes footage.

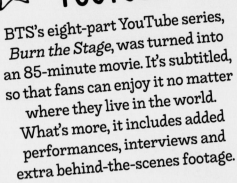

ONE MOVIE PRESS RELEASE SAID:

"A journey of **40 CONCERTS** across **19 COUNTRIES** with more than **550,000** roaring audience members, making history that gave wings to seven boys." The two-minute trailer clocked up more than one million views on YouTube in just one day.

MOST-WATCHED GROUP ON YOUTUBE

They've bagged **10 BILLION** views across **800 VIDEOS** on their Bangtan TV channel.

SUPER BOWL?

"I'm just throwing it out there," Suga said in October 2018, "but maybe we could perform at the Super Bowl someday." Cross all of your fingers and toes right now, peeps!

WHAT NEXT?

Now that we've celebrated the stuff BTS have achieved so far, it's time to talk about what's coming up. If their history is anything to go by, the next few years are going to be off the scale for our K-pop kids.

STADIUM TOUR

The rumours are true. BTS are on tour, and it's guaranteed to be just as awesome as it sounds. The tour kicked off in LA. It began just after their new EP was released!

NEW EP

Fill your ears with the most recent BTS beats...

It was their third number one hit on the Billboard 200 chart. Here's all you need to know about it.

When is it?
It's happening in 2019!

What's it called?
Map of the Soul: Persona

What's it called?
Love Yourself: Speak Yourself

When did it come out?
12 April 2019!

It's the follow up to *Love Yourself: Answer*, which was released in 2018.

It is their 7th studio album.

Where are they headed?
It's a WORLD tour!

Jung Kook

BTS are a burst of kaleidoscopic colour, and they've well and truly refreshed the music industry. It's easy to see why the band has fans all over the world. They're more than just singers and dancers – BTS are role models. They're a symbol of freedom, and they make good things happen.

Fans especially love how open they are when it comes to talking about their emotions. The band have confided: "We would be lying if we said there wasn't any pressure in front of us, but we manage to get over it by openly talking about it with one another all the time. As you might know, we've been living together in the same house for the last five years, and we share literally everything, even if it is stress and burden. BTS teamwork helps us get through the pressure and expectation in everyday life, and it also lets us stay humble as ordinary people – like guys next door. We make casual jokes and give pieces of advice to other members so that we can still be down-to-earth, as we were before BTS."

And that is why BTS are the best!

K-POPOGRAPHY

To new members of BTS's ARMY, the group's back catalogue of albums, EPs, singles, tours and TV shows can seem pretty complex. The band release music in themed trilogies or series. We hope this K-popography will help you keep your collection up to date...

KOREAN ALBUMS
2 COOL 4 SKOOL (12 June 2013)
DARK & WILD (19 August 2014)
WINGS (10 October 2016)
LOVE YOURSELF: TEAR (18 May 2018)
LOVE YOURSELF: ANSWER (24 August 2018)

BTS aren't your typical boy band. There is **SO** much more to them than just their music! These guys **TRULY CARE** about their **FANS** – they **INTERACT** with them on **SOCIAL MEDIA** and even **DEDICATE SONGS** to them.

GUESS WHAT?

RM collaborated with **FALL OUT BOY** and featured on the remix of their song **CHAMPION**.

REISSUE ALBUMS
SKOOL LUV AFFAIR SPECIAL ADDITION (14 May 2014)

YOU'LL NEVER WALK ALONE (13 February 2017)

JAPANESE ALBUMS

(Re-packaged Korean albums, in Japanese, with additional songs)

WAKE UP (24 December 2014)

YOUTH (7 September 2016)

MIC DROP/DNA/CRYSTAL SNOW (6 December 2017)

FACE YOURSELF (4 April 2018)

EPS

O!RUL8,2? (11 September 2013)

SKOOL LUV AFFAIR (12 February 2014)

THE MOST BEAUTIFUL MOMENT IN LIFE, PART 1 (29 April 2015)

THE MOST BEAUTIFUL MOMENT IN LIFE, PART 2 (30 November 2015)

LOVE YOURSELF: HER (18 September 2017)

MAP OF THE SOUL: PERSONA (12 April 2019)

TOURS

2014–2015 BTS LIVE TRILOGY EPISODE II: THE RED BULLET

2015 BTS 1ST JAPAN TOUR WAKE UP: OPEN YOUR EYES

2015 BTS LIVE THE MOST BEAUTIFUL MOMENT IN LIFE ON STAGE

2016 BTS LIVE THE MOST BEAUTIFUL MOMENT IN LIFE ON STAGE: EPILOGUE

2017 BTS LIVE TRILOGY EPISODE III: THE WINGS TOUR

2018 BTS WORLD TOUR: LOVE YOURSELF

2019 BTS WORLD TOUR: LOVE YOURSELF: SPEAK YOURSELF

COOL COLLAB

WALE and **RM** met through **TWITTER**, and together the pair worked on a **HIP-HOP** track called **CHANGE**.